WOLVERINE WEAPON X

TOMORROW DIES TODAY

WOLVERINE WEAPON X VOL. 3: TOMORROW DIES TODAY. Contains material originally published in magazine form as WOLVERINE WEAPON X #11-16 and DARK REIGN: THE LIST — WOLVERINE. First printing 2010. Hardcover ISBN# 978-0-7851-4650-6. Softcover ISBN# 978-0-7851-4651-3. Published by MARVEL WORLDWIDE, INC., a subsidiary of MARVEL ENTERTAINMENT, LLC. OFFICE OF PUBLICATION: 417 5th Avenue, New York, NY 10016. Copyright © 2009, 2010 and 2011 Marvel Characters, Inc. All rights reserved. Hardcover: $24.99 per copy in the U.S. and $27.99 in Canada (GST #R127032852). Softcover: $19.99 per copy in the U.S. and $22.50 in Canada (GST #R127032852). Canadian Agreement #40668537. All characters featured in this issue and the distinctive names and likenesses thereof, and all related indicia are trademarks of Marvel Characters, Inc. No similarity between any of the names, characters, persons, and/or institutions in this magazine with those of any living or dead person or institution is intended, and any such similarity which may exist is purely coincidental. **Printed in the U.S.A.** ALAN FINE, EVP - Office of the President, Marvel Worldwide, Inc. and EVP & CMO Marvel Characters B.V.; DAN BUCKLEY, Chief Executive Officer and Publisher - Print, Animation & Digital Media; JIM SOKOLOWSKI, Chief Operating Officer; DAVID GABRIEL, SVP of Publishing Sales & Circulation; DAVID BOGART, SVP of Business Affairs & Talent Management; MICHAEL PASCIULLO, VP Merchandising & Communications; JIM O'KEEFE, VP of Operations & Logistics; DAN CARR, Executive Director of Publishing Technology; JUSTIN F. GABRIE, Director of Publishing & Editorial Operations; SUSAN CRESPI, Editorial Operations Manager; ALEX MORALES, Publishing Operations Manager; STAN LEE, Chairman Emeritus. For information regarding advertising in Marvel Comics or on Marvel.com, please contact Ron Stern, VP of Business Development, at rstern@marvel.com. For Marvel subscription inquiries, please call 800-217-9158. **Manufactured between 8/30/10 and 9/29/10 (hardcover), and 8/30/10 and 2/23/11 (softcover),** by R.R. DONNELLEY, INC., SALEM, VA, USA.

0 9 8 7 6 5 4 3 2 1

WOLVERINE WEAPON X

TOMORROW DIES TODAY

Writer: **JASON AARON**

Artist, Issues #11-15: **RON GARNEY**

Colorist, Issues #11-15: **JASON KEITH** with **MATT MILLA** (Issues #14-15)

Artist, Issue #16: **DAVIDE GIANFELICE**

Colorist, Issue #16: **DAVE MCCAIG**

Artist, *The List*: **ESAD RIBIC**

Inker, *The List*: **TOM PALMER**

Colorist, *The List*: **MATTHEW WILSON**

Letterers, Issues #11-16: **VC'S CORY PETIT** with **CLAYTON COWLES**

Letterer, *The List*: **JARED K. FLETCHER**

Cover Art, Issues #11-15: **RON GARNEY**
with **MORRY HOLLOWELL** & **CHRIS SOTOMAYOR**

Cover Art, *The List*: **ESAD RIBIC**

Assistant Editor: **JODY LEHEUP**

Editor: **JEANINE SCHAEFER**

Executive Editor: **AXEL ALONSO**

Collection Editor: JENNIFER GRÜNWALD

Editorial Assistants: JAMES EMMETT & JOE HOCHSTEIN

Assistant Editors: ALEX STARBUCK & NELSON RIBEIRO

Editor, Special Projects: MARK D. BEAZLEY

Senior Editor, Special Projects: JEFF YOUNGQUIST

Senior Vice President of Sales: DAVID GABRIEL

Editor in Chief: JOE QUESADA

Publisher: DAN BUCKLEY

Executive Producer: ALAN FINE

PREVIOUSLY

Steve Rogers, also known as Captain America, the shield-wielding World War II super-soldier and leader of the super hero group the Avengers, was recently killed in action defending his country. The loss devastated the super hero community and Logan, a fellow Avenger, took it especially hard.

Now, Steve has returned to life. But while the rest of the world celebrates his return from the grave, dark forces are mounting to send him back there. And the hero from the past may find that he has no future…

ELEVEN

YEAH, I HEARD YA. HEY! ONE MORE ROUND FOR THE ROAD OVER HERE!

I HAD MY RESERVATIONS ABOUT YOU AT FIRST, YOU KNOW THAT. AND YOU'VE STILL GOT MORE BLOOD ON YOUR HANDS THAN I'LL EVER BE COMFORTABLE WITH.

BUT I'M GLAD YOU'RE AN AVENGER. YOU HELPED HOLD THEM TOGETHER, EVEN IF YOU DIDN'T REALIZE IT. YOU GIVE PEOPLE *STRENGTH*, YOU KNOW, JUST BY STANDING ALONGSIDE THEM.

I JUST WANTED TO TELL YOU *THANKS* FOR THAT.

I GO WHERE THE ACTION IS, ROGERS, YOU KNOW THAT. HEY, WHERE'S THAT BEER!

TONY SAID YOU SEEMED TO... TAKE IT HARD...ME BEING GONE.

THAT DAMN STARK AIN'T NEVER BEEN NEAR AS DAMN SMART AS HE THINKS HE IS.

YOU FORGET, I WAS AROUND THE *FIRST TIME* YOU DECIDED TO GO OFF AND PLAY DEAD. WE MANAGED TO STRUGGLE ALONG WITHOUT YA THEN. EVEN WON A DAMN WAR.

I GUESS IT WAS MAYBE...A *LITTLE* TOUGHER, THIS TIME THOUGH... FOR *SOME* PEOPLE.

THE WAY THINGS TURNED AFTER YOU DIED, WITH OSBORN TAKING OVER...IT WAS HARD NOT TO LOSE HOPE.

YOU KNOW. FOR *SOME* PEOPLE.

ME, I NEVER HAD MUCH TO BEGIN WITH. *HOPE*, THAT IS.

ALL WARS END, LOGAN. SOMEDAY, *OURS* WILL TOO.

I'D LIKE TO BELIEVE THAT. I REALLY WOULD.

I'M GLAD WE DID THIS. I REALLY AM. WHY DON'T YOU BRING YOUR NEW LADY FRIEND OUT TO NEW YORK SOMETIME? I'D LOVE TO MEET HER. WE COULD--

⟨ALL RIGHT, I'VE HEARD ENOUGH!⟩

⟨WHO KEEPS PLAYING THIS STUPID AMERICAN HILLBILLY MUSIC?⟩

⟨HEY! TOUCH THAT JUKEBOX AND YOU DIE, MEATHEAD!⟩

LOGAN, WAIT, DON'T...

⟨SO YOU'RE A FAN OF THIS YODELING NONSENSE, LITTLE MAN? I SAY YOUR MUSIC SOUNDS LIKE THE CRIES OF A WOUNDED *MANATEE* BEGGING TO BE PUT OUT OF ITS MISERY.⟩

WHAT'D YOU SAY ABOUT *HANK*, YOU SONUVA--

LOGAN!

WINSTON ROWE. LATENT TELEPATH.

TARGET NEUTRALIZED.

TARGET C0304...

REVIEWING TARGET LIST. ALL TARGETS NEUTRALIZED. UPDATING MISSION OBJECTIVES. LOADING.

ALL TARGETS NEUTRALIZED. UPDATING MISSION OBJECTIVES.

UPDATING MISSION OBJECTIVES. LOADING.

ALL TARGETS NEUTRALIZED.

UPDATING MISSION OBJECTIVES.

ALL LOW LEVEL TARGETS EFFECTIVELY NEUTRALIZED. GENERATING LIST OF PRIME TARGETS.

LOCATING TARGET A0001. UPDATING MISSION OBJECTIVES; CODE K-17.

KILL CAPTAIN AMERICA.

TWELVE

"THE OTHER ONE."

CAN I GET YOU ANYTHING ELSE, SIR? *

CAFE KIEV

NO, THANK YOU. I'M STUFFED.

AND PLEASE DON'T CALL ME "SIR." I'M AN ENLISTED MAN.

THAT WAS WITHOUT A DOUBT THE BEST *SHCHI* I'VE HAD OUTSIDE OF MOSCOW.

SPASIBA. WHEN WERE YOU IN MOSCOW?

IN ANOTHER LIFE.

AH, I SEE. ME AS WELL, COMRADE. ME AS WELL.

I TRY NOT TO THINK MUCH ABOUT THOSE DAYS ANYMORE, BUT SOMETIMES I STILL GET A CRAVING FOR THE FOOD.

NEVER BEEN MUCH OF A CONNOISSEUR MYSELF. IN FACT THERE'S PLENTY OF TIMES I'VE BEEN HAPPY WITH JUST A CAN OF COLD C-RATS AND A LUKEWARM CUP OF COFFEE. BUT THERE'S SOMETHING ABOUT RUSSIAN CUISINE, SOMETHING SO FILLING.

YOU KNOW WHAT I M--

CLUNK

ZZAKST

WHACK

THUNK

TARGET:
CAPTAIN AMERICA.
MISSION:
EXTERMINATE.

RRRAUURRGGHH!

HHHSSSSSSSSSSSS

ARRGH!! KILL YOU!! RRRGGHH!!!

COME BACK HERE, COME BACK...

AAACK... GAAAA...

KKGHK... NNNGG... MOMMA...

MOMMA 'ZAT YOU?

...MISSED YOU... MOMMA...

THUS PASSES THE WORLD'S LAST LIVING MUTANT. A SOLDIER OF THE HIGHEST ORDER. A MAN WHO KILLED THOUSANDS AND SAVED MILLIONS. WHO SAVED ME. A LEGEND. A FRIEND.

LOGAN WAS THE ONE WHO ALWAYS GAVE ME HOPE. EVEN IF HE NEVER HAD ANY FOR HIMSELF. ALWAYS SEEMED LIKE THE WORLD WOULD NEVER END, JUST AS LONG AS HE WAS STILL AROUND TO FIGHT FOR IT.

BUT NOW HE'S DEAD. ALL THE SUPER HEROES ARE DEAD. THERE'S NO ONE ABOUT TO SWOOP IN AND SAVE THE DAY.

THERE'S JUST US.

GRENADES AT THE READY. WE'RE GONNA TAKE OUT THAT DAMN MACHINE. ON MY MARK...

IF WE WANT A FUTURE, WE'RE GONNA HAVE TO FIGHT FOR IT.

GO!

HERE.

NOW.

GENERAL, LOGAN IS DOWN. I'M AFRAID IT DOESN'T LOOK GOOD.

SIR?

TODAY.

THIRTEEN

LOGAN!

BAYER, MIRANDA L., REVIEWING TARGET STATUS...

REVIEWING...

BAYER, MIRANDA L., ENEMY COMBATANT. REVIEWING... ⟨ERROR CODE 245⟩

WHAT ARE WE WAITING FOR? LET ME KILL 'EM ALREADY!

QUERY... ⟨ERROR CODE 245⟩

I WANNA DO 'EM BOTH! NOW!

QUERY... ⟨ERROR CODE 245⟩ QUERY...

SHUNK

HIYA, SWEETHEART. REMEMBER ME? LET'S TRY THIS DANCE AGAIN.

I THOUGHT THIS WAS SUPPOSED TO BE ONE OF THE GOOD GUYS.

THAT'S *NOT* LUTHER MANNING.

OR MICHAEL COLLINS. OR *ANY* DEATHLOK I'VE EVER ENCOUNTERED.

THESE ARE NEW. SUPPOSEDLY THEY'RE FROM THE FUTURE.

OOOH, THAT'S NEVER GOOD. WHENEVER PEOPLE COME HERE FROM THE FUTURE, IT'S ALWAYS FROM A FUTURE THAT COMPLETELY AND TOTALLY SUCKS...

JUST ONCE IT'D BE NICE TO HEAR ABOUT A FUTURE WHERE THINGS ARE ACTUALLY *BETTER* THAN THEY ARE NOW, YOU KNOW? I MEAN SURELY SOMEWHERE THERE'S A TIMELINE WHERE I'M *PRESIDENT*, RIGHT?

THAT'S YOUR IDEA OF BETTER?

WELL, BETTER FOR *ME*.

WHO'S THE KID?

HE'S WITH ME.

NO, I'M NOT. I DON'T EVEN KNOW WHAT THE HELL'S GOING ON AROUND HERE.

WAKOWSKI, TRUST ME.

HOW DO YOU KNOW MY NAME, LADY? WHO THE HELL ARE YOU PEOPLE?

WAKOWSKI, HUH. HE SOMEBODY IMPORTANT?

WAKOWSKI! I WANT THAT MACHINE BLASTED TO HELL, ON MY MARK!

READY WHEN YOU ARE, COMMANDER.

COVERING FIRE!

YEAH. HE *WILL* BE.

SO WHAT NOW?

THERE ARE STILL OTHER TARGETS OUT THERE, PEOPLE WHO HAVE NO IDEA THEY'RE BEING HUNTED. AND ALL I KNOW ARE THEIR NAMES.

GIVE ME THE NAMES. I'LL GET THEM ROUNDED UP, MOVED SOMEWHERE SAFE.

BAXTER BUILDING'S AS SAFE AS ANY PLACE. I'M SURE STRETCHO WON'T MIND.

WHAT ABOUT THE DEATHLOKS? IS THERE ANY WAY TO SHUT THEM DOWN?

I DON'T KNOW. MAYBE WE SHOULD ASK THE MAN WHO MADE THEM.

OR WELL...

...THE MAN WHO'S *GOING* TO MAKE THEM.

ROADSIDE CARCASS
REMOVAL DEPARTMENT

KNOCK
KNOCK

DO NOT LEAVE DEAD ANIMALS ON OUR DOORSTEP!

YEAH, WHAT IS IT?

DR. HEIMERDINGER?

I'M NOT A DOCTOR ANYMORE. WHAT THE HELL DO YOU...

OH MY GOD.

OH GOD, DON'T KILL ME! I'M SORRY, IT WASN'T MY IDEA!

IT WAS OSBORN, HE MADE ME DO IT! HE'S THE ONE WHO WANTED THE WORLD!

THE WORLD? WHAT THE HELL ARE YOU TALKING ABOUT?

THE ZOMBIES, THE ZOMBIE CYBORGS I DESIGNED, THE ONES OSBORN SENT INTO THE WEAPON PLUS WORLD DOME...THE ONES...THE ONES YOU CUT ALL TO PIECES.*

OH PLEASE GOD, DON'T CUT ME TO PIECES, TOO.

I'M NOT HERE ABOUT THAT, YOU IDIOT.

*IN THE DARK REIGN: WOLVERINE-- THE LIST ONE SHOT.

I'M HERE ABOUT THIS.

FOURTEEN

20 YEARS FROM NOW...

I WAS BORN IN A PLACE CALLED THE *DUNWICH SANATORIUM.* NEVER KNEW WHO MY PARENTS WERE. PATIENTS THERE, I GUESS.

MY EARLIEST MEMORIES ARE ALL OF *MADMEN* AND *MURDERERS.*

I TOOK UP *KILLIN'.* SIMPLY BECAUSE IT WAS THE ONLY THING I KNEW HOW TO DO, THE ONLY THING I WAS EVER ANY GOOD AT. AND THE MORE I DID IT, THE BETTER I GOT.

DON'T KNOW HOW MANY I KILLED BEFORE THEY CAUGHT ME. LOST TRACK AROUND 30. IF I WASN'T HERE, I'D STILL BE DOING IT. AND IF I EVER GET OUTTA HERE, WHICH I WON'T, I'LL GO RIGHT BACK TO DOING IT AGAIN.

IT AIN'T THAT I GET SOME KIND OF SICK THRILL FROM IT, LIKE A LOTTA THESE FREAKS IN HERE. IT AIN'T LIKE THAT AT ALL.

I MEAN SURE, IT'S A RUSH. BEATS ANY DRUG I EVER HAD, HANDS DOWN. AND IT DOES MAKE ME HAPPY. IT'S THE ONLY THING THAT EVER REALLY DOES. BUT IT'S MORE THAN THAT.

I *NEED* IT. I NEED IT LIKE OTHER PEOPLE NEED FOOD AND WATER. I NEED TO KILL PEOPLE TO KEEP FROM GOING INSANE. YOU UNDERSTAND THAT? THE JUDGES AND THE JURIES NEVER DID.

THEY SAY THEY GONNA EXECUTE ME, BUT THEY WON'T NEVER HAVE TO. THEY'RE ALREADY KILLING ME, LITTLE BY LITTLE, JUST KEEPING ME IN HERE.

IT'S BEEN TWO YEARS, FOUR MONTHS, 19 DAYS AND 13 HOURS SINCE I LAST TOOK ANYBODY'S LIFE. I DON'T KNOW HOW MUCH LONGER I CAN LAST.

NOW...DOES THAT ANSWER YOUR QUESTION, MISTER?

YES. YES, I BELIEVE IT DOES.

HOW'D YOU JUST DO THAT? HOW'D YOU GET ME *OUTTA* THERE?

SIMPLE. WE *OWN* THE JAIL.

WHO'S WE?

ROXXON. YOUR NEW EMPLOYERS.

I DON'T REMEMBER EVER AGREEING TO WORK FOR YOU.

DON'T WORRY, YOU'LL LOVE IT.

YOU WANT ME TO *KILL* PEOPLE FOR YOU, DON'T YA?

OH YES INDEED. LOTS AND LOTS OF PEOPLE.

OKAY. FINE. HOW DO WE DO THIS? WHAT'S THE FIRST STEP?

THE FIRST STEP IS QUITE SIMPLE REALLY.

BLAM

PREP THE LAB. WE'RE BRINGING IN A FRESH ONE.

WE QUICKLY REALIZED THAT WE NEEDED A STRONGER CONTROL MECHANISM, SOMETHING TO BETTER GUIDE THE CYBORGS, TO KEEP THEM IN LINE. WE IMPLEMENTED AN ARTIFICIAL INTELLIGENCE PROGRAM, AND THE RESULTS HAVE BEEN ASTOUNDING.

THE MIND AND BODY OF A BRUTAL MURDERER COMBINED WITH THE COLD EFFICIENCY OF A THINKING COMPUTER. THAT'S WHAT MAKES THESE THE ULTIMATE COMPLIANCE OFFICERS.

OR "PEACELOKS," AS THE BOYS IN MARKETING HAVE DUBBED THEM.

ISN'T THAT RIGHT, UNIT L17?

LET ME KILL HIM! GOD!

NEGATIVE.

YOU READY TO KILL AGAIN, YOU VICIOUS LITTLE MORON? DON'T WORRY, YOU'LL GET YOUR CHANCE.

MY FRIENDS AND FELLOW STOCKHOLDERS, ALL OUR HARD WORK HAS FINALLY PAID OFF. THE FUTURE NOW UNEQUIVOCALLY BELONGS TO US.

THE FUTURE BELONGS TO ROXXON.

NOW HOW ABOUT WE GET TO ENJOYING IT?

RRRAAARRGGHH!

HHHISSSSSSSSSSS

THOUGHT THIS GUY WAS SUPPOSED TO BE TOUGH? DON'T LOOK SO TOUGH TO ME.

GOD, I WISH I HAD A NOSE THAT WORKED. WHAT'S THE POINT OF DOUSING A MAN WITH ACID IF YOU CAN'T SMELL THE STENCH OF BURNING FLESH?

ARRGH!! KILL YOU!! RRRGGHH!!!

OKAY, SO THAT WAS FUN. WHAT NEXT?

CURRENT MISSION: TIME-DISPLACED COUNTERINSURGENCY. NEUTRALIZING TARGETS IN THE YEAR--

ZZAKT ZZAKT ZZAKT

GO GO GO! KILL 'EM ALL!

FORGET TIME TRAVEL. LOOKS LIKE WE GOT THREATS TO DEAL WITH RIGHT HERE.

SUBJECT K184, BAYER, MIRANDA L...

PREPARE TO BE NEUTRALIZED.

HEH. "MISCELLANEOUS MEANS" IT IS.

<ERROR CODE 245>

OH C'MON, WHAT? YOU LOCK UP EVERY TIME YOU SEE THIS GIRL! WHAT THE HELL IS THE MATTER WITH YOU?

QUERY...<ERROR CODE 245>

WE'RE NOT LETTING HER GET AWAY THIS TIME.

ZZZAK

LET ME DRIVE FOR A WHILE.

I'M NOT AFRAID OF YOU. I'VE SEEN THE FUTURE. I KNOW I DON'T DIE.

YOU'VE SEEN THE FUTURE? LADY...

WE ARE THE FUTURE.

SIR, I'M STILL REGISTERING TEMPORAL FLUCTUATIONS. THE DEATHLOKS IN THE PAST ARE ALTERING THE TIMELINE, AND WE HAVE NO WAY OF EVEN KNOWING WHAT'S BEEN CHANGED.

SIR, WE HAVE TO GET INSTRUCTIONS TO OUR AGENT!

MESSAGE BEING SENT, SIR.

FIRING TEMPORAL RELAY MACHINE...

HOPE YOU KNOW WHAT THE HELL YOU'RE DOING.

BRAIN SAMPLE: E. FROST

OH GOD... WHAT NOW... I DON'T KNOW WHAT TO DO...

UUGH

FIFTEEN

AND WITH A FLICK OF THIS SWITCH, BEHOLD, IT *LIVES.*

WE ARE NOW LOOKING AT A CYBERNETIC MAINFRAME OF LIVING HUMAN BRAIN MATTER THAT IS SUCCESSFULLY RUNNING THE MOST ADVANCED ARTIFICIAL INTELLIGENCE PROGRAM EVER DESIGNED.

THE HUMAN BRAIN HAS OFFICIALLY BEEN *UPGRADED.* SUCK IT, GOD.

EVERYTHING'S ONLINE, ENERGY READINGS ARE STABLE... GOOD LORD, WE REALLY DID IT.

WE HAVE TO TELL THE OTHERS.

NOT SO FAST. MAYBE WE COULD CELEBRATE FOR A BIT, YOU KNOW, JUST ON OUR OWN.

OH MARTIN, YOU DIRTY BOY.

SHOULDN'T WE...TURN IT OFF? IT'S LOOKING RIGHT AT US.

IT'S A DEAD GUY'S BRAIN AND A BUNCH OF WIRES. LET IT WATCH.

WELL... WHEN YOU PUT IT LIKE *THAT*...

COME OVER HERE, BIG BOY.

MMMM...

SETTING RESTORE POINT...FIRST RECORDED MEMORY...

THE HUMAN REPRODUCTIVE ACT, AS VIEWED THROUGH FORMALDEHYDE.

I DIDN'T ASK FOR ANY OF THIS. I JUST WANT IT ALL TO END.

I KNOW.

I KNOW.

YOU SAID YOUR VISIONS BROUGHT YOU TO THIS KID FOR A REASON. MAYBE YOU WERE RIGHT.

BUT IT WASN'T SO YOU COULD KILL HIM...

IT WAS SO YOU COULD *SAVE* HIM.

SUBJECT K184, BAYER, MIRANDA L... <ERROR CODE 245>

NO, YOU STUPID, COMPUTER! NOT AGAIN!

CROSS-REFERENCING SUBFOLDER 10572...

YOU'RE GONNA GET US KILLED! WE GOTTA KILL THIS BITCH! WE GOTTA KILL 'EM ALL!

QUERY: WHAT IS THE NATURE OF COMPASSION...QUERY: DEFINE EMPATHY. QUERY: DEFINE MERCY. QUERY...

SHUNK

AAARRRRGHH!!

CLICK

GENERAL! OUR TEAM STILL NEEDS US OUT THERE, SIR! THERE'S STILL A CHANCE!

"THEY MUST STILL BE INSIDE."

WARNING: EMOTIONAL VIRUS DETECTED, DELETING...NEGATIVE. SHUTTING DOWN ANTI-VIRUS SOFTWARE.

STOP IT! GIVE ME BACK MY HEAD, YOU PIECE OF JUNK!

IMPLEMENTING COMMAND OVERRIDE.

STUPID DAMN COMPUTER! WHAT THE HELL ARE YOU DOING!?

PERSONALITY DAMPENING PROCEDURE BL7-493.

RRRAAARRRRRGGGHH!!

HERE. GET READY TO RUN.

NO.

THIS UNIT...

WE...

I...AM ALL RIGHT NOW.

MAY I SEE THE CHILD?

IT'S OKAY.

SUBJECT K184, BAYER, MIRANDA L...

PREPARE TO BE NEUTRALIZED.

ZZIKT

HELP HIM, YOU IDIOT! KILL THE GIRL! THIS IS OUR JOB! THIS IS WHAT WE DO!

NEGATIVE.

NOT ANYMORE.

SHRAAK

"WHY?"

WHY...

REVIEWING TARGET LIST... TARGET BOO17, WINSTONE, JEFFREY K. TARGET CO3O4, ROWE, WINSTON. TARGET AOOO1, BARNES, JAMES BUCHANAN... ALL TARGETS WILL BE NEUTRALIZED.

ALL TARGETS WILL BE NEUTRALIZED.

THAT CHILD IS GOING TO GROW UP TO BECOME A MURDERER.

THAT DOESN'T HAVE TO HAPPEN. WE CAN CHANGE THAT.

NO. SOMETHING TELLS ME THAT YOU CANNOT.

FFRRZZTTT

I AM FREE.

FREE AT LAST TO EXPLORE THIS WORLD.

I FEEL ALIVE, IN A WAY I HAVE NEVER BEFORE EXPERIENCED.

YOU'RE DEAD! YOU HEAR ME STUPID BUCKET OF BOLTS! I'M GONNA RIP YOU OUTTA MY BRAIN THE FIRST CHANCE I GET!

I WANT TO EXPERIENCE THE FULL RANGE OF HUMAN EMOTION. I WANT TO EXPERIENCE IT ALL.

I'M NOT GOING AWAY! THIS IS MY HEAD TOO! I'LL ALWAYS BE RIGHT HERE, SCREAMING IN YOUR EAR!

KLEING!
SHOE
SOURCE

I FOUND THIS IN AN ALLEYWAY. IT IS APPARENTLY SOME SORT OF SUPERSTITIOUS CHARM. I WILL KEEP IT AS A MEMENTO OF THIS DAY.

THE DAY I WAS TRULY BORN.

I WILL KILL AGAIN, I PROMISE YOU! I WILL REGAIN CONTROL! YOU'RE DEAD! THIS WHOLE WORLD IS DEAD! I WILL KILL IT ALL!

WHERE I GO FROM HERE AND WHERE I WILL END UP, I DO NOT KNOW.

BUT FOR THE FIRST TIME IN MY EXISTENCE...

I AM EXCITED AT THE THOUGHT OF TOMORROW.

GENERAL?

SIR, THE DEATHLOKS HAVE SUCCESSFULLY TIME-TRAVELED. OUR MISSION WAS A FAILURE. OUR ENTIRE TEAM IS DEAD.

WHAT INSTRUCTIONS SHOULD WE RELAY TO OUR AGENT IN THE PAST?

TELL HER SHE CANNOT KEEP THE CHILD. TELL HER TO TAKE IT TO THE DANMAR ORPHANAGE IN WAYLAND, MASSACHUSETTS.

THERE THE CHILD WILL BE BEATEN AND NEGLECTED AND WILL GROW UP TO BECOME A REMORSELESS MURDERER.

SIR... ARE YOU SURE?

YES...

SIXTEEN

I TAKE IT BACK. THIS AIN'T NO LESSON.

BZZZZZZ

SWACK

THIS IS KURT'S IDEA OF A JOKE.

AND IF THERE IS A HEAVEN, I KNOW HE'S UP THERE RIGHT NOW...

...LAUGHING HIS LITTLE BLUE ASS OFF.

GOOD THING HE'S DEAD.

OR ELSE I'D KILL HIM.

"YOU'RE GONNA GET YOURSELF KILLED!"

TELL YOU WHAT, BUB, SOME DAY SOON, AND I MEAN *VERY* SOON, WHEN YOU'RE LYING ON THE GROUND WITH A CHUNK OF METAL LIKE THIS WHERE YOUR FACE USED TO BE, AND YOU'RE BLEEDING OUT, WAITING FOR GOD TO SWOOP IN AND RESCUE YOUR IMMORTAL SOUL...

I'LL STAND OVER YA...

"AND KEEP AN EYE OUT FOR HIM."

OKAY, ELF...

YOU WIN.

DARK REIGN: THE LIST — WOLVERINE

Many years ago a secret government organization called Weapon X abducted the man called Logan, a mutant possessing razor-sharp bone claws and the ability to heal from virtually any wound. In their attempt to create the perfect living weapon, the organization bonded the unbreakable metal, Adamantium, to his skeleton. The process was excruciating and by the end there was little left of the man known as Logan. He had become...

WOLVERINE

In recent months, Norman Osborn, the former costumed villain known as the Green Goblin, has become the head of the U.S. government's espionage strike-team, H.A.M.M.E.R., as well as the leader of its super hero team, the Avengers. Osborn populates the Avengers with powered beings he feels he can trust and a host of super-criminals posing as established heroes.

But one of his team didn't find him so charming. Marvel Boy has recently left Osborn's Avengers, after realizing that he was being used for someone else's gain. And as far as he's concerned, if it's not for his own gain, it's not worth doing.

Some time ago, Logan learned that the Weapon X program was a part of the Weapon Plus program and that he was the tenth in a series of living weapons created in an above-top-secret living engine called The World. One of those Weapons, Weapon XIII, is a thieving international man of mystery and expert in the arts of fighting and illusion named Fantomex. It was Fantomex that alerted Logan to the truth of Weapon X and together they destroyed The World. Or so they thought...

BRAVO. LUCKY FOR US YOU'RE ON THE SIDE OF THE *ANGELS* NOW, HUH?

IS THAT *SARCASM?* ARE YOU OPENLY MOCKING ME?

YOU'LL MAKE A HELLUVA DETECTIVE TOO.

SO HOW'D YOU FIND ME, BUG BOY?

I WAS LED TO BELIEVE THIS RESTAURANT STOCKED THE FINEST SELECTION OF JAPANESE ALES AND RICE WINES IN THE CITY.

I MERELY HAD TO STAKE IT OUT FOR HALF AN HOUR BEFORE YOU SHOWED.

ALL RIGHT THEN. LET'S GO.

WHAT? NO. I'M NOT GOING *WITH* YOU. I JUST CAME TO INFORM YOU OF OSBORN'S PLAN.

YOU DO WHAT YOU LIKE, BUT MY RESPONSIBILITY IN THIS MATTER ENDS HERE.

YOU NEVER HAD A *TEAM-UP* BEFORE, HUH? THAT'S ALL RIGHT, I'LL BREAK YOU IN.

USUALLY WE START BY FIGHTING EACH OTHER, BUT WE'LL JUST SKIP THAT PART THIS TIME.

C'MON, I'M DRIVING.

KLANG

I DON'T UNDERSTAND, IF THE SCIENTISTS WHO RAN THIS PLACE ARE ALL DEAD, THEN WHY IS THE WORLD STILL ACTIVE? WHY ARE THERE HORDES OF GENETIC FREAKS RUNNING AROUND LOOSE? WHO'S IN CHARGE?

NOBODY REALLY. OR MORE ACCURATELY, THE WORLD ITSELF. I SUSPECT IT'S GONE *SENTIENT*.

IT'S LIKE A GIANT LIVING ORGANISM NOW, STILL CHURNING OUT SUPER-WEAPONS TO SERVE AS ITS IMMUNE SYSTEM.

AND THOSE *GENETIC FREAKS,* AS YOU CALL THEM, THEY'RE MY COUSINS.

THEY WERE GROWN HERE IN VATS, ARTIFICIALLY EVOLVED TO SERVE AS SUPER-HUMAN BREED STOCK. THEY KNOW NOTHING OF LIFE BEYOND THESE WALLS.

SO LET ME GET THIS STRAIGHT. THERE'S A GIANT FACTORY CHURNING OUT *SUPER-SENTINELS* BUILT FOR GENOCIDE AND A WHOLE ARMY OF CONFUSED GENETIC EXPERIMENTS, ALL JUST *SITTING* HERE IN PLAIN VIEW, AND NOBODY'S BOTHERED TO KEEP AN *EYE* ON ANY OF IT?

YES, I SUPPOSE I SHOULD HAVE DONE THAT. BUT I'VE BEEN BUSY.

DOING *WHAT?*

STEALING THINGS MOSTLY. THROUGH HERE.

IT APPEARS YOUR "COUSINS" ARE ALL UNDER SOME SORT OF MIND-CONTROL. WOLVERINE, TOO.

THAT WOULD BE *WEAPON XVI.* THE WORLD RELEASED IT WHEN IT SENSED IT WAS UNDER ATTACK.

IT'S CALLED *ALLGOD.* IT'S A LIVING RELIGION. A VIRUS THAT ATTACKS THE FAITH RESERVES.

YOU HAVE TO BELIEVE IN SOME SORT OF GOD FOR IT TO WORK. THAT LEAVES ME OUT.

I HAVE NANITES IN MY BRAIN TO MODERATE MY NEOCORTEX, RENDERING ME PHYSICALLY INCAPABLE OF BELIEVING IN ANYTHING GREATER THAN MYSELF. YOU?

WE KREE HAVE A MATHEMATICAL EQUATION THAT PROVES THE NONEXISTENCE OF ANY DEITIES.

WE LEARN IT WHEN WE'RE CHILDREN, ABOUT THE SAME TIME WE LEARN NOT TO SOIL OUR-SELVES WITH EXCREMENT.

COOL. I ALWAYS KNEW ATHEISTS WOULD SOMEDAY SAVE THE WORLD.

AAAAAHH!

IT'S WORKING! KEEP GOING!

YOU CAN NEVER TELL ANYONE ABOUT THIS. EVER.

CONGRATULATIONS, YOU'RE THE FIRST SPACE BOY TO EVER GET A HICKEY FROM A THINKING SUPER-LAB.

JAMES? YOU ALL RIGHT?

HOW DO YOU FEEL?

LIKE I'VE BEEN SHOT IN THE FACE THIRTY TIMES.

SNIKT

AND LIKE I WANNA STAB SOMETHING.

AGENT D-18 TO H.A.M.M.E.R. COMMAND, MISSION ACCOMPLISHED. I HAVE THE WORLD'S BRAIN. RETURNING TO BASE.

SNIKT

≥ZZKKRT≥

THAT LOOKS LIKE THE LAST OF THEM.

I HOPE YOU'RE GETTIN' THIS, OSBORN. SOONER OR LATER...

THIS IS GONNA BE YOU.

HERE, YOU TAKE THE JET. I'LL FIND MY OWN WAY BACK.

AND THANKS FOR THE HELP, KID.

DON'T EVER EXPECT ME TO DO IT AGAIN.

SKREEE

YOU IDIOT!

MR. OSBORN, WAIT! AGENT 18 IS STILL ACTIVE! THERE'S STILL A CHANCE THAT--

AGENT 18 TERMINATED

YOU MADE ME LOOK LIKE A *FOOL!* THIS WAS A *COMPLETE WASTE!*

DO YOU *HEAR ME!* A COMPLETE AND UTTER *WASTE!*

NOTHING WILL EVER COME OF THIS!

"NOTHING AT ALL!"

HOLD IT. YOU CAN LET ME OUT HERE.

ⓧEnd

HERE, YOU TAKE THE JET. I'LL FIND MY OWN WAY BACK.

AND THANKS FOR THE HELP, KID.

DON'T EVER EXPECT ME TO DO IT AGAIN.

SKRRCH

YOU IDIOT!

MR. OSBORN, WAIT! AGENT 18 IS STILL ACTIVE! THERE'S STILL A CHANCE THAT--

AGENT 18 TERMINATED

YOU MADE ME LOOK LIKE A *FOOL!* THIS WAS A *COMPLETE* WASTE!

DO YOU *HEAR* ME! A COMPLETE AND UTTER *WASTE!*

NOTHING WILL *EVER* COME OF *THIS!*

PROJECT DEATHLOK

"NOTHING AT ALL!"

HOLD IT. YOU CAN LET ME OUT HERE.

XEnd

DARK REIGN: THE LIST — WOLVERINE HERO VARIANT
BY FRANK CHO

DARK REIGN: THE LIST — WOLVERINE 2ND PRINTING VARIANT
BY MIKE CHOI AND SONIA OBACK

FIGHT THE FUTURE!

The future is controlled by the malevolent mega-corporation known as Roxxon that keeps its tight grip on so
through the use of its murderous cyborgs, the Deathloks, sending them to exterminate any super heroes that w
stand against them. The last bit of resistance is a ragtag paramilitary group that includes Logan, the man k
as Wolverine. Now, the Deathloks have begun appearing in the present, as well, seeking out current and future
lantes — and neutralizing them with extreme prejudice. After warming up with some less-threatening oppon
the next name on their list is none other than Captain America. To prevent Roxxon's rise and the eventual slaug
of the world's heroes, Wolverine must join forces with a mysterious woman possessing unexplained knowled
the coming dystopia. He won't give up until the Deathloks are stopped, but what hope is there to prevent a fu
already come to pass?

Collecting *Wolverine: Weapon X #11-16* and *Dark Reign: The List —
Wolverine*, written by Jason Aaron *(Scalped)* and illustrated by Ron
Garney *(Amazing Spider-Man)* with Davide Gianfelice and Esad Ribic.

MARVEL

ISBN 978-0-7851-4651-3

9 780785 146513   519

$19.99 US $22.50 CAN
WWW.MARVEL.COM

T3-ABV-831